Contents

KU-032-738

Inside and out 4

Why I need to be healthy 6

Keeping clean 8

Looking after your hair 10

Brushing your teeth.........................12

Eating well 14

Exercising...............................16

Keeping safe.............................18

Sleeping 20

What can go wrong? 22

Avoiding germs............................24

Preventing diseases.........................26

The whole body............................28

Find out for yourself 30

Glossary 31

Index...............................32

Any words appearing in bold, **like this**, are explained in the Glossary.

Inside and out

Everyone prefers to feel well rather than ill. When you are healthy, you are wide awake and full of energy. When you are ill or unhealthy, you may feel tired and not want to do much. You can help yourself to stay healthy by keeping yourself clean, sleeping well, eating healthy food and taking plenty of exercise.

This boy is full of energy and looks healthy. He probably looks after himself.

My Amazing Body

STAYING HEALTHY

THE COLLEGE OF WEST ANGLIA

Angela Royston

www.raintreepublishers.co.uk
Visit our website to find out more information about **Raintree** books.

To order:
☎ Phone 44 (0) 1865 888112
🗎 Send a fax to 44 (0) 1865 314091
💻 Visit the Raintree bookshop at **www.raintreepublishers.co.uk** to browse our catalogue and order online.

First published in Great Britain by Raintree,
Halley Court, Jordan Hill, Oxford OX2 8EJ,
part of Harcourt Education.
Raintree is a registered trademark of Harcourt
Education Ltd.

Editorial: Nick Hunter and Catherine Clarke
Design: Kim Saar and Roslyn Broder
Illustrations: Will Hobbs
Picture Research: Maria Joannou
Production: Jonathan Smith

Originated by Dot Gradations Ltd
Printed and bound in China by South China
Printing Company

ISBN 1 844 43388 9 (hardback)
08 07 06 05 04
10 9 8 7 6 5 4 3 2 1

ISBN 1 844 43395 1 (paperback)
09 08 07 06 05
10 9 8 7 6 5 4 3 2 1

British Library Cataloguing in Publication Data
Royston, Angela.
Staying Healthy. - (My Amazing Body)
613
A full catalogue record for this book is available from
the British Library.

Acknowledgements
The publishers would like to thank the following
for permission to reproduce photographs:
Alamy Images p. **28**; Bubbles p. **6**, Corbis pp. **17**
(Ariel Skelley), **18** (Richard Hutchings), **19**; FLPA pp.
10 (Jurgen and Christine Sohns), **21** (Foto Natura), **25**
(Martin B. Withers); Gareth Boden p. **24**; NHPA p. **9**
(Laurie Campbell); Pete Morris p. **4**; Punchstock pp.
13, **20**, **23**; Science Photo Library pp. **5** (Zephyr), **7**
(Alfred Pasieka), **11** (Gaillard Jerrican), **12** (BSIP), **14**
(Mazimillian Stock Ltd), **15** (Susan Leavines), **16**
(Mehau Kulyk), **22** (Mauro Fermariello), **26** (Josh
Sher), **27** (Saturn Stills); Tudor Photography p. **8**.

Cover photograph of an X-ray of a healthy human
heart, reproduced with permission of Science Photo
Library and of children playing reproduced with
permission of Corbis.

The publishers would like to thank Carol Ballard
for her assistance in the preparation of this book.

Every effort has been made to contact copyright
holders of any material reproduced in this book.
Any omissions will be rectified in subsequent printings
if notice is given to the publishers.

The paper used to print this book comes from
sustainable resources.

Inside your body

How healthy you are depends on what is happening inside your body. You rely on different **organs**, such as your **lungs**, **liver** and **heart**, as well as your blood, to keep you alive. When you are healthy, these organs work well. When you are unhealthy, some do not work so well.

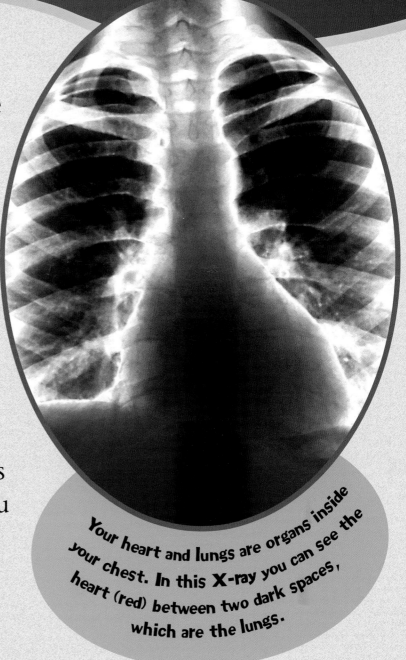

Your heart and lungs are organs inside your chest. In this **X-ray** you can see the heart (red) between two dark spaces, which are the lungs.

Healthy dog

You can often tell whether a dog is healthy just by looking at it. Its eyes are bright, its nose is wet and its fur is shiny.

Why I need to be healthy

Your body and your brain work better when you are healthy. It is easier to think and concentrate at school when you feel well.

Even if you are usually healthy, you may become ill from time to time. You can become ill when your body is invaded by **germs**. If you are healthy your body will soon fight off these germs. Looking after your health can stop many germs getting into your body in the first place.

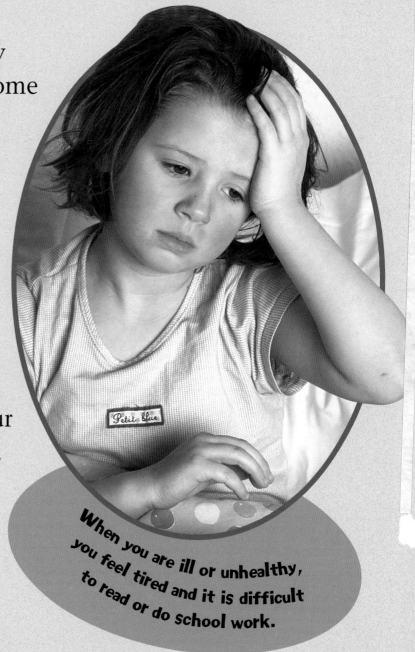

When you are ill or unhealthy, you feel tired and it is difficult to read or do school work.

Germs

Germs are all around you – in the air, on your hands and almost everything. Germs, such as bacteria and viruses, are tiny living things that are too small to see unless you look at them under a **microscope**.

Some germs get inside your body through your nose or mouth, or through a cut. Most germs affect a certain part of the body. Some affect your stomach and make you vomit.

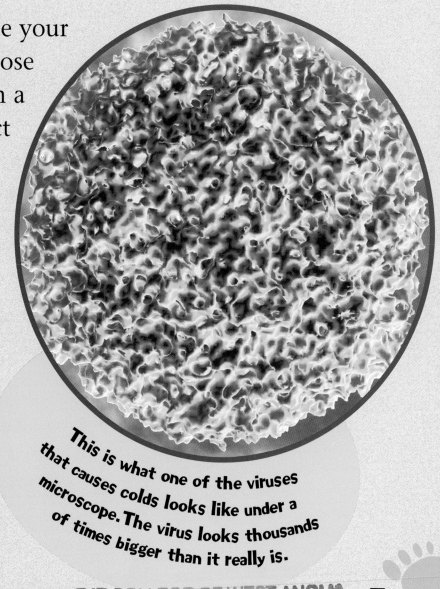

This is what one of the viruses that causes colds looks like under a microscope. The virus looks thousands of times bigger than it really is.

Keeping clean

Dirt contains lots of **germs** so it is important to keep yourself clean. You should wash your whole body every day or two, either by having a bath or shower. Washing cleans your skin and helps get rid of germs before they make you ill.

Use soap and clean water to wash your hands. Using soap will wash away more dirt and germs than water on its own.

Washing your hands

It is particularly important to wash your hands before you eat. Germs spread very easily from your hands on to the food you touch and eat. Toilets are covered with germs, so make sure you wash your hands after using the toilet.

A cat cleans itself by licking its fur. It washes its ears by licking one of its paws and rubbing it across its ears.

Clean clothes

Germs also live in spilt food, sweat and other dirt that gets into your clothes as you wear them. Clean clothes smell fresh and are better for you than dirty ones.

Bird bath

Birds like to bath in a pool of water, but sometimes they cover their feathers with dust. The dust helps to remove tiny insects in their feathers.

Looking after your hair

Whether you have short or long hair, curly or straight hair, you need to keep it clean and tidy. Combing or brushing your hair makes it neat and stops it **irritating** your eyes. Washing your hair with shampoo removes dirt and makes your hair shiny.

Animal grooming

Animals with hair, **groom** their fur to keep it clean. Fleas and other insects live in the fur of animals. The insects bite the animal's skin and make it itchy.

Monkeys like to groom each other's fur. When they find an insect, they eat it!

Head lice

Humans sometimes get insects in their hair, too. Even if your hair is perfectly clean, it is hard to avoid catching head lice because they move easily from one person's head to another.

Head lice bite your head and lay their eggs in your hair. You need to use a special shampoo or oil to get rid of them.

When you wash your hair, use shampoo to get all the dirt out and rinse your hair well to get rid of all the shampoo.

Smart birds

Birds use their beaks to groom and comb their feathers. Grooming keeps the feathers smooth so that the bird can fly through the air better.

Brushing your teeth

To keep your teeth healthy, you need to brush them every day. If you do not brush your teeth, they will **decay**. Do not eat or drink too many sweet things, because sugar is bad for your teeth.

Tooth decay

Your teeth are amazingly strong, but **germs** in your mouth can damage them. Germs feed on sugar left in your mouth and make a smelly substance called plaque.

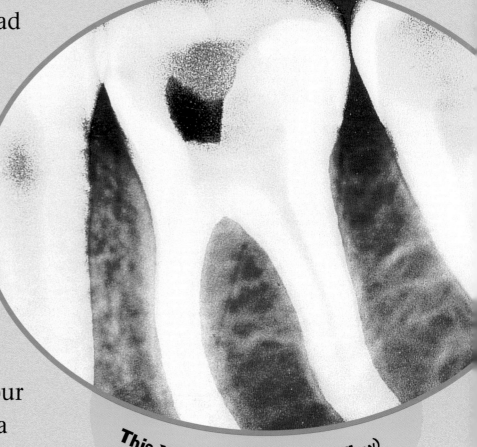

This X-ray shows a tooth (yellow) with a hole (black) in it.

12

Plaque sticks to your teeth and gums. As the germs feed, they make **acid**, which can burn a hole in the hard surface of your teeth. If the hole becomes deep, it will give you toothache.

Healthy teeth

Brushing your teeth with toothpaste removes the sugar and germs. You should also try to visit a dentist about every six months to check that your teeth are healthy.

Brush your teeth from the gums to the tips – fronts and backs!

Bad breath

Animals do not need to clean their teeth because they do not eat or drink sugar. But animals that eat meat often get bits stuck between their teeth. As the meat rots, it makes their breath stink!

Eating well

Your body needs water and many different kinds of food to stay healthy. Food gives you energy, makes you grow and helps your body to work properly.

Lots of different kinds of food are healthy. More than half the food you eat should be energy food and fruit and vegetables.

Healthy food

Food such as bread, potatoes, pasta and rice are the best foods to give you energy. Sugar and fat also give you energy, but it's best not to eat a lot of them. Sugar is not good for your teeth and too much fatty food can make you fat. Meat, fish, cheese, eggs and beans help your body to grow, so eat some of them every day. Eat plenty of fruit and vegetables, too. They contain **chemicals** and **fibre** that your body needs to work well.

Drinking water

You lose water when you **urinate**, sweat and breathe out. You need to drink plenty of water every day to replace the water you lose.

The food you swallow goes into your stomach and intestines, where it is broken down into different chemicals. The chemicals your body needs pass through the wall of the intestines into your blood.

Exercising

Exercise makes your **muscles** and **joints** stronger. It also strengthens your **heart** and **lungs**. To be fit and healthy you should exercise at least three times a week for around 20-30 minutes. If you don't exercise, your heart and other parts of your body will not work so well.

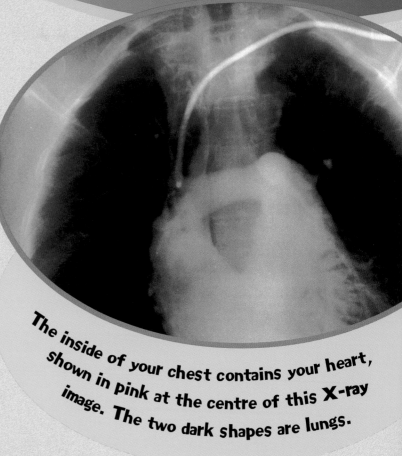

The inside of your chest contains your heart, shown in pink at the centre of this X-ray image. The two dark shapes are lungs.

Exercising muscles and joints

Muscles are the soft parts of your body that cover your bones and make them move. Your ankles, knees, hips, shoulders and elbows are some of the joints in your body. Walking, dancing and swimming all exercise your joints and muscles by moving them.

Exercise that makes you puff

When you exercise hard, you begin to puff and breathe in extra air. Air contains **oxygen**, which our muscles need to work. Oxygen passes through your lungs into your blood, and your heart pumps blood to your muscles. So when your muscles work hard, your heart and lungs have to work hard too. This makes them stronger.

Pets need exercise

Pets need regular exercise too. Some hamster cages have a wheel that the hamster can run around. Large cages can have networks of tunnels for them to run along.

This boy and dog are having fun and exercising at the same time. The longer they play, the fitter they will be.

Keeping safe

Sometimes when you are exercising you fall and hurt yourself. You may scrape your knee or bang your head. The faster you are moving, the more you hurt yourself if you fall. When you ride a bicycle or skate you should protect yourself by wearing a helmet and protective pads.

You should always wear a cycle helmet when you ride a bicycle.

Pads and helmet

A cycle helmet protects your head in case you have an accident. The helmet soaks up most of the **force** of the bang. People who ride horses or ponies also wear a hard helmet and thick clothes in case they fall off. If you roller skate or skateboard, you should protect your elbows and knees with special pads.

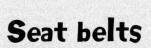

A crab's hard shell is like a suit of armour, covering its body, legs and pincers.

Seat belts

When you travel by car, you should always wear a seat belt. The belt stops you flying forward if the car stops suddenly.

Animal armour

A tortoise has a hard shell to keep it safe. Its body is always protected inside the shell. If the tortoise is in danger, it pulls its head and legs in too.

Sleeping

Most children need to sleep for about 10 –12 hours every night. As you grow older, you do not need so much sleep. Adults should sleep for about 7 hours every night.

Sleeping is a habit

Your body soon gets used to falling asleep at about the same time every night. You probably have to get up at a certain time to get to school. So make sure you go to bed early enough to fit in the number of hours of sleep that you need.

When you are asleep your muscles and other parts of your body rest. Your mind relaxes too. When you wake up in the morning you will feel fresh and rested.

This cat is having a nap, but any noise or movement nearby will wake it up immediately.

Irregular sleep

If you do not sleep well at night, you will feel tired during the day. Being tired makes it difficult to think at school. You are also likely to be bad tempered and not have the energy to enjoy playing with your friends.

Cat napping

Many animals, such as cats, sleep lightly and have several short naps during the day instead of a long sleep at night.

What can go wrong?

Everybody catches **germs** sometimes. Germs are all around you and you cannot help breathing them in. If your body is healthy though, and you look after yourself when you are ill, you will soon get better.

Fighting germs

Your body has several ways of fighting germs. **Saliva** kills some of the germs you put in your mouth, and your stomach kills off more germs. Hairs and **mucus** in your nose stop some germs getting into your body. Your body's main weapon against germs, though, are special **cells** in your blood. These cells kill germs.

Sometimes when you are ill, you need to see a doctor. This doctor is using an otoscope to look inside the boy's ear.

Looking after yourself

Having a high **temperature** is one sign that you are ill. An adult can take your temperature using a thermometer. When you are ill, you may need to rest and sleep more than usual. This allows your body to concentrate on killing germs.

If you are very ill, a doctor may give you medicine to help you get better. Be sure to take the medicine exactly the way the doctor tells you to, and never take someone else's medicine.

When you are ill your parents or doctor may take your temperature, to see if it is higher than normal.

Avoiding germs

Many illnesses are caused by **germs** passed from one person to another. You can do some things to avoid catching germs. You can also avoid passing germs on to other people. One of the best ways to keep your germs to yourself when you are ill is to stay at home, if you can.

Used tissues are full of germs, so do not leave them lying around.

Keep colds to yourself!

Every time you sneeze or cough, you could catapult millions of germs into the air around you. Always cover your mouth when you cough, and sneeze into a tissue. Don't leave dirty tissues lying around – the germs will just float into the air. Spitting also spreads germs. If you need to spit, make sure you spit into a tissue and then throw it away.

Avoiding stomach upsets

You can avoid swallowing germs that will make you sick by washing your hands before you eat. Make sure that the food you eat is clean and fresh. If food is left uncovered, flies may land on it and **infect** it with germs.

Animals have germs in their mouths and on their bodies. Wash your hands after stroking or holding a pet and do not let it lick your face.

Preventing diseases

Some **germs** can make you seriously ill. Different **vaccinations** can stop you catching most of these germs. A vaccination increases the special **cells** in your blood that fight certain **diseases**. Some diseases, such as chicken pox, still cannot be **prevented** with a vaccine.

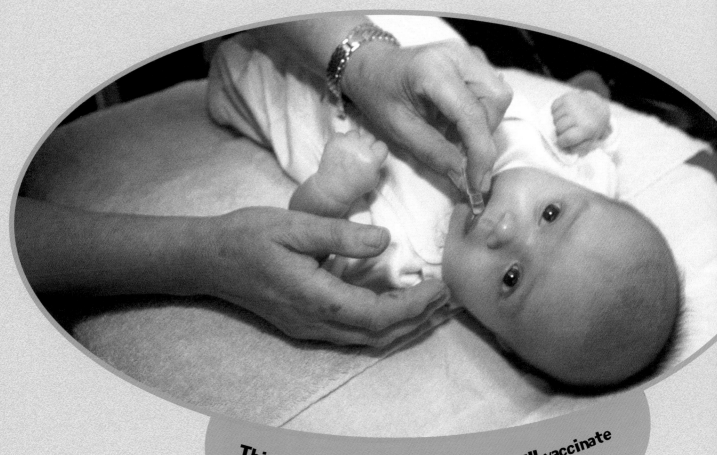

This baby is being given drops that will vaccinate it against polio. Polio is a disease that stops some of your muscles from working.

Jabs and drops

You may have been given vaccinations when you were a baby and before you started school. Vaccinations protect you against polio, whooping cough, measles and many other diseases. The polio vaccine is given as drops straight into your mouth, but most vaccines are **injected** into your blood through your skin.

Medical check-ups

Most young children have a medical check-up from time to time. A doctor checks that they are growing well and tests how well they see and hear. If your eyes do not work as well as they should, the doctor can arrange for you to have glasses. If there is a problem with any part of your body, the doctor will try to fix the problem.

This girl is being given an injection that will stop her catching a disease called rubella.

The whole body

Being healthy affects the whole of your body. Your body is made up of millions of tiny **cells**. Each cell needs **oxygen** all the time from the air you breathe in, and **nutrients** from the food you eat. If you do not eat enough healthy food, your cells will not get enough of the nutrients they need to work properly.

The healthier you are, the higher you can jump to catch a ball! These children are full of energy and their bodies are fit and healthy.

Exercise

Exercise helps your whole body as well as your **muscles** and **joints**. When you exercise, your **heart** pumps faster. This means that all of your cells get more oxygen and nutrients, from your blood.

Helping your brain and other organs

Your brain works best when you have slept well and when it gets plenty of oxygen. Drinking enough water helps your brain and kidneys to work better. The **liver** and kidneys take out harmful **chemicals** and waste from the blood. The better they do this, the better you feel.

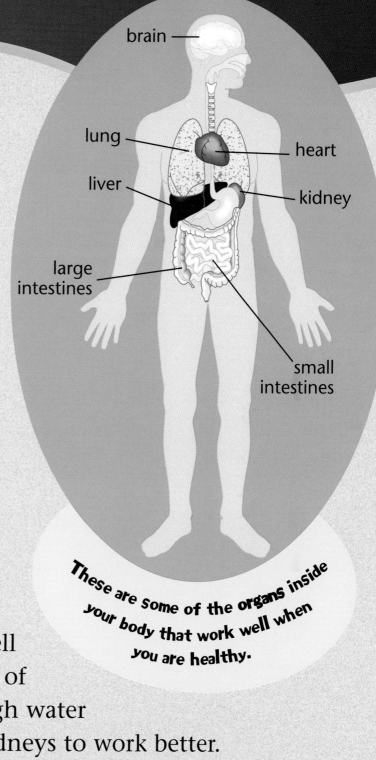

brain

lung

liver

large intestines

heart

kidney

small intestines

These are some of the organs inside your body that work well when you are healthy.

29

Find out for yourself

Everybody's body is slightly different but they all work in the same way. Find out more about how your own amazing body works by noticing what happens to it. What happened to your body the last time you had a cold? If you have had head lice, how did you get rid of them? How often do you need to exercise? You will find the answers to many of your questions in this book, but you can also use other books and the Internet.

Books to read

Why does my body smell? And other questions about hygiene, Angela Royston (Heinemann Library, 2002)

Health matters: Hygiene and your health, Jillian Powell (Hodder Wayland, 2002)

Using the Internet

Explore the Internet to find out more about staying healthy. Websites can change, but if some of the links below no longer work, don't worry. Use a search engine, such as www.yahooligans.com or www.internet4kids.com, and type in keywords such as 'bones', '**muscles**' and 'exercise'.

Websites:

www.kidshealth.org contains lots of information about how your body works and how to stay healthy

www.bbc.co.uk/science/humanbody/body contains an interactive body and lots of information. Click on skeleton and muscles to find out more about bones and moving.

www.brainpop.com gives links to many science websites for kids. Click on 'health' for quizzes and films about different parts of the body, including bone structure and broken bones.

Disclaimer

All the Internet addresses (URLs) given in this book were valid at the time of going to press. However, due to the dynamic nature of the Internet, some addresses may have changed, or sites may have ceased to exist since publication. While the author and publishers regret any inconvenience this may cause readers, no responsibility for any such changes can be accepted by either the author or the publishers.

Glossary

acid liquid with a sour, bitter taste

cell smallest building block of living things

chemical substance that makes up other substances

decay rot

disease illness

fibre parts of plants that humans cannot digest. Fibre helps your digestive system to work well.

force power or impact

germ tiny form of life that can make you ill. Germs are so small you need a microscope to see them.

groom keep clean and take care of

heart special muscle in your chest that pumps blood around your body

infect when germs grow in living things

inject push into the body, often through a needle in the skin

irritate annoy or itch

joint place where two or more bones meet and fit together

liver part of the body that helps process digested food and breaks down harmful chemicals in the blood

lungs parts of the body that take in oxygen when you breathe in and get rid of waste carbon dioxide when you breathe out

microscope instrument that makes very tiny things look large enough to see

mucus liquid that lines some tubes inside your body, such as your nostrils and breathing tubes

muscles parts of your body that you use to move

nutrients chemicals in food that your body needs to get energy and stay healthy

organ part of the body, such as the heart, brain and stomach, that has a particular job to do

oxygen gas that living things need to survive

prevent stop

saliva liquid made in the lining of your mouth

temperature how hot or cold something is

urinate get rid of waste water from the body

vaccinate help the body fight a particular germ by using a small dose of the germs

X-ray kind of photograph that shows parts of the inside of your body, such as your bones

Index

accidents 18, 19
animals 5, 9, 10, 11, 13, 17, 19, 21, 25

brain 6, 29

cells 22, 26, 28, 29
clothes 9
colds 7, 25
coughs and sneezes 25
cycle helmets and pads 18, 19

dirt 8, 9

energy 4, 14, 15, 21, 28
exercise 16–17, 18, 28, 29
eyesight and hearing 27

food 9, 12, 14–15 25, 28

germs 6–7, 8, 9, 12, 13, 22, 13, 24,
    25, 26

hair 10–11
hand washing 8–9, 25
head lice 11
heart 5, 16, 17, 29

illness 4, 6, 7, 22–25, 26, 27

joints 16, 29

liver and kidneys 5, 29
lungs 5, 16, 17

medical check-ups 27
medicines 23
muscles 16, 17, 20, 28, 29

nutrients 28, 29

oxygen 17, 28, 29

plaque 12–13

safety 18–19
seat belts 19
sleeping 20–21, 23, 29
spitting 25
stomach upsets 7, 25

teeth 12–13
teeth, brushing 13
temperature 3
tiredness 4, 6, 21
toilet 9
tooth decay 12–13

vaccinations 26–27
viruses 7

washing 8–9, 10, 11, 25
water 15, 29
whole body 28–29